Start Your
SOCIAL MEDIA
MANAGEMENT
BUSINESS
NOW!

Start Your
SOCIAL MEDIA MANAGEMENT
BUSINESS
NOW!

EZRA DANJUMA AKAMA

Start Your Social Media Management Business
Ezra Danjuma Akama

COPYRIGHT © 2022

Published and printed in Nigeria by

Emergence Publishers
Kaduna-Nigeria
+2348066429711 theemergencelinks@gmail.com

All rights reserved

Emergence Publishers
...connecting ideas with reality

DISCLAIMER

The word social media in the English language refers to social networks. In this book however, the word - social media continues to be used without regards to grammar structure to render it as a plural word. Note that the word is used in this book as one of the technological efforts of man to connect humans anywhere in the world irrespective of their physical location.

That said, if you look forward to making money from social media, there are different ways to do so. You can sell products. You can sell training. You can sell newsletter subscriptions. You can sell service.

Whichever you decide to do, it is work. This book is not a magic wand, the money is in the work you put in.

Dedication

To every young person who legitimately seeks ways he or she can make money offering service online.

You deserve to make money online.

CONTENTS

Social media puts the 'public' into PR and the 'market' into marketing.

Chris Brogan

PREFACE

Some years ago, my friends and I went to buy 'time' to log on and surf the internet and catch some fun on Yahoo mail before the 30 minutes of time we bought elapsed in the Internet Cafè around the neighbourhood. Yes, we would pay for 30 minutes only because it was what was affordable then, in fact, 15 minutes was what we could afford sometimes.

Interestingly, we visited these Cafè only on weekends. It means we surfed the internet only once in 7 days. What we knew as social media was Yahoo mail, nothing more.

In recent, the concept of social media has rapidly evolved from what we knew it and what it is now. From being an activity we spent less than an hour on in a week to what we do almost as frequently as the tick of the clock tocks.

'...almost as frequently as the tick of the clock tocks?' Is that sentence even correct? Ignore the correctness of the sentence and focus on the message.

Truth be told, social media has evolved from just being a platform for the connection of humans. Today, we breathe social media. I mean, our lives have come to practically depend on it and I will tell you what I mean. I have only tried to imagine how life is for the men I hear who do not have personal accounts on social media like Warren Buffet, and Joshua Selman.

Social media connects brands and customers, service providers and clients, employers and employees, boo and bae, teachers and students, pastors and members, and the list is endless.

Let me tell you one secret. There's no better time to begin your social media management business than now. A lot of people are not aware that it is the business of the now and the future.

this is why if you go to your search box on Google to

search for businesses or skills of the future, I can bet that you will not find social media management.

I will give you one reason why social media will become a business that will experience a rush. People are increasingly busy and social media is increasingly seeking their presence and dominance at the same time. They will be faced with the pursuit of the desires of life and the pursuit of dominance and influence on social media. One must be careful not to think that a balance can be achieved. One must suffer, either in life's pursuit or on social media.

If you are not convinced by what I have said, how about you see it as the desire to get assistance? Just like anyone in business, a time comes when a need for professionals arises to help with handling certain areas where he expects effectiveness and proficiency.

People hire the services of social media management agencies because they need professional and reliable service. You can become that professional and reliable business.

INTRODUCTION

At this point in my life, I can say for sure that I have grown beyond cajoling and sweet-talking people to buy anything I sell, including the services I offer.

I say it all the time. Anyone who bought anything from me and comes to a point of being so sure it was not worth his or her money, the person should be kind enough to courteously request a refund and I will oblige. First, I believe everyone has a right to request a refund, but that right is not the same as the right to be rude. I needed to state the 'courteous' part. It applies to this book.

Isn't this a good opening remark? Of course, it is.

It helps both of us. You can now read the book with a consciousness of measuring the value and relevance of the content. If you finish reading and you are convinced that it wasn't worth your money, ask for a refund.

On my part, giving you such a guarantee puts me on my toes to expect that someday, someone (and that person may be you) may request a refund. If that happens, it will mean I need to sit up and revise my work.

But wait, were you expecting a regular book introduction. This book, 'Starting your Social Media Management Business,' is not your regular book. Business books are not regular books.

This one, in particular, would not just tell you what to do, it tells you how to do it. It gives you links where needed. It gives you some examples that should help boost your morale in knowing that some people are doing similar businesses, including yours truly, and we are still in business. If we can, you can, too.

In this book, I bared it all. Where you needed to get extra resources or help, the book says it. No hard feelings.

On second thought, if this book is a 200-page book, you would probably be among the people that will say it's too bulky. Now I have provided you with a small book with plenty of details. Magical, right?

Let me confess. I avoided things like social media ads. The Facebook ad, for example, is a complete world on its own. Alone, it can make up a book. Not to talk about other ads. But the good news is that I explained every alternative other than a Facebook ad.

While I remain open-minded and expect to hear just ANYTHING from you, it is my earnest desire that you read the book for the benefit of you and me. Are you surprised? When you read my book, I benefit from your reading too. Don't ask how, just read...

Let's dive in.

Why Social Media Manager

I will provide you with some stats. I think it is a good place to start.

In the first quarter of 2021, Facebook users hit 2.85 billion. That is more than the entire population of the second-largest continent in the world – Africa which contains 54 countries. Can we now say that Facebook is a continent on its own?

What about WhatsApp? There are over 2 billion active users. That is more than the most populous country in the world, and that would be China. Could we also say that WhatsApp is like Facebook, a country of its own? Not just any country, but the most populous.

Now imagine that the users of Facebook and WhatsApp are combined. They will both form a figure that is higher than the most populous continent (Asia) in the world. Asia contains nearly 60% of the world's population.

What does 60% of the world's population mean to you? If you are a user of both Facebook and WhatsApp, this figure is something you should think about.

Chat-Banking

I have asked you questions and I just realized that I am going to ask you more questions probably because this chapter is titled as a question itself.

Another question. Why does chat banking focuses mainly on Facebook and WhatsApp?

I will attempt to join you in answering this question and I guess it is cool. These banks which have introduced chat banking have stopped seeing these figures (2.85 billion and 2 billion) as something that should be compared with the population of countries and continents. Yes, that is tricky you would say. Don't you think?

The banks see social media platforms as market places and the number of people on these platforms they see as customers (or potential customers at least). They, as corporate organizations, therefore, tasked themselves with the responsibility of providing chat banking on social media to serve their customers and convert new customers.

Social Gathering or Potential Market

Now, over to you. How do you see the over 1 billion people on Instagram?

A social gathering or a potential market?

In less than 5 years, TikTok too has over 1 billion active users. What do you make out of that? For me, I would say a huge market.

Let me point this out. Social media, as its name implies, is a media (channels) of socialization. This is why each social medium (like Facebook, Tiktok, etc.) has its basic structure primarily patterned around helping people have a great time meeting and socializing with new friends and old ones alike.

Truth is, social media is still a platform for social gatherings. Just that, it is a platform for social gathering and more to some people. Other people see it as a market. You should too.

It is so important that you understand that how people see social media is a fundamental requirement for building any business structure around it.

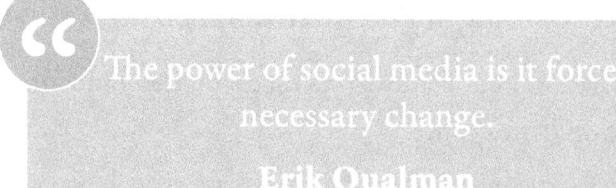

> **"** The power of social media is it forces necessary change.
>
> **Erik Qualman**

Online Presence

If social media was a location where anyone could physically go and receive money, everyone would sleep and wake there just to cash out money from it, but it is not so. It is a virtual location where anyone can have a 24-hour active presence if they so desire.

Today's reality is forcing everyone to have an active online presence. With those figures of active users on social media, it is a clear indication that a good chunk of people's attention has moved and is now found online.

We don't have to debate about this. Don't you think?

People spend more time on social media than they do in any physical market.

People spend more time on social media than they do in their academics.

People spend more time on social media than they do sports.

How about cooking? Reading? Dancing? Racing? Sleeping? Social media will win this debate in its favour every time.

Social Media Management

Today, people have social media presence. For some, it is intentional; and the others it is just fun. For this reason, it is increasingly becoming pertinent for corporate organizations to usurp the opportunity they see in the people who are on social media, especially the category of people who are unintentional about being on social media.

Wait a minute let me break it down and make the point. Anybody can be on social media for fun but corporate organizations cannot afford to do that. The stakes are not the same. The difference between these two groups is management. Management is what guides individual and corporate behaviours in any environment.

Apart from corporate organizations, any person who is intentional about being on social media platforms is consciously or unconsciously building a personal brand. In whatever case, management is what is common between the person and corporate organizations on social media.

Managers are Busy People

Seeing that you are already acquainted with the context within which the word *management* is used in this chapter, you would thus agree with me that the group of people whose behaviour in the social media environment is guided must be busy enough not to have so much time to keep an active social media presence. It is the same with corporate organizations, an active online presence is a luxury they cannot afford.

6

Before I go on, I bet you don't know who this book is written for because I didn't tell you in the introduction.

Anyone who has a social media presence because he or she can afford the time required to maintain an online presence, they deserve to make money and that is why I wrote this book. I primarily wrote it for them.

As we continue, I will get to you the other set of people who would find this tremendously useful to them.

Since managers are busy, who then is not?

Social *Gatheree*

The social gatheree is the one who is on social media for fun. To them, social media is a social gathering. A virtual location to reunite with old friends; an opportunity to meet their next boyfriend or girlfriend; a place to cool off while waiting for the bus or train; etc.

All these things they do for fun are also things they do for free. However, they must see this as the opportunity to turn what they do for free (spend their time for fun on social media) into what they can do for a fee (by becoming social media managers).

How? You may ask.

Truth is that it is becoming extremely difficult for the managers to independently combine their offline and online activities and get all their desired results.

Look at this scenario:

A CEO has a company to run. Amongst the many things he needs to do to ensure his business stay afloat, he has a wife to love and children to father, he also has mentors to learn from and protégés to impart.

Now there is a Facebook account to his name, a Facebook page to the company's image, and maybe Instagram and LinkedIn. How about WhatsApp (or Telegram) and Twitter?

How is he supposed to attend to all these people and these things every day? He needs help, surely.

He would get help only if the social gatheree is

willing to step in to help him take care of the things that can be outsourced like managing his social media handles and pages. He cannot outsource the responsibility to learn from his mentors nor his role in the lives of his protégés. He cannot outsource his responsibility on the home front to love his wife or be a father to his children.

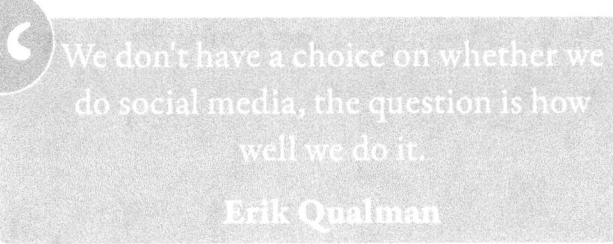

> We don't have a choice on whether we do social media, the question is how well we do it.
>
> Erik Qualman

A Business of Time

I know you are already considering how you can begin. Let me continue with my questioning, don't be tired yet.

How much time do you spend online daily? Even if you have never tried to make a count or keep a record, now that I have asked you, I want you to make an attempt and come up with an estimated number of hours.

According to the Guardian, the average Nigerian

spends about four hours and five minutes on social media daily.

The first requirement for starting a social media management business is time. The stats above suggest is that four hours and five minutes is average for people but not you, if you are interested in the business of social media management.

So, let's talk about the social media management business.

The Social Media
Management Business

What is social media management about and how can the money be made from it? This is the question, anyone, reading this book to this point, I believe, should be asking.

The truth is that this is about the time a lot of young people should learn how to make money from the several little things they overlook especially the time spend on social media.

One question that is pertinent for us to answer is: what is social media management?

Social media management is about taking up the

responsibility to help manage, market, and handle social media accounts of busy professionals and social media pages of businesses or high-net-worth individuals.

> We get to live in a time that we get to use social media as a tool.
>
> **Gigi Hadid**

Social media managers offer expert service. You need to understand this. There are three dimensions to social media management:

1. Social Media Engager

2. Social Media Manager

3. Social Media Marketer

All these three are closely related but they're very much different from one another. They are three distinct services.

1. Social Media Engager

This implies everything that pertains to responding to direct messages (DMs), replying to comments, followers' queries, etc.

Essentially, it means ENGAGING with fans or followers of a page or account.

Most engagements are prompted by content. People make more comments on content they come across than they send direct messages to inquire about a content.

Hence, the question is who creates the content?

Let me give you a simple example so you will have a sneak peek of how this thing works.

Think about product reviews. The person who publishes a product like an app or website would usually be different from the person who would respond to the engagements the product draws.

For an app or website, an engager is needed to respond to people's reviews or queries and questions after the app or web developer is published and running.

On a general note, when some corporations do a product launch, usually they would need a Social Media Engager to respond to people's messages or queries and comments concerning that product.

Individual influencers too need a Social Media Engager to respond to comments and messages on their pages. I'm sure you know by now that most influencers do not manage their pages (or business account), they probably manage their accounts though. Yes, there is a difference between a personal account and a page (like a business account).

I'm letting you understand this so that if you're taking up a job from a client, you need to be sure that the job description is clearly defined so that you don't shortchange yourself or allow yourself to be underpaid.

2. Social Media Manager

This involves creating content and making posts. Two daunting tasks beset every social media manager.

- *Creating content*: It involves creating content in text, picture-graphics, or video formats. This is because, by implication, it means that some special skills are quite necessary. Basically, skills in graphics

14

design and video editing.

One of the most powerful tools everyone must learn is 'scheduling posts.' Scheduling posts works on pages. On Facebook, I create and schedule posts that go live on their accord based on the date and exact time I set. My scheduled posts go live automatically and this affords me rest for weeks.

Search for 'Business Suite,' it is free. This tool is quite popular amongst many people. You should explore it. Another option, though advanced is Hootsuite or Buffer. These advanced tools are not free.

When it comes to the job of a social media manager, managers charge clients based on how much content they desire to be created and posted daily or weekly. The nature of the posts too, whether, text, graphics, or videos is a factor.

Invariably, it means that if you're interested in becoming a social media manager, what you spend on learning graphics design or video editing is important only because of the guarantee that you'd get it back soon after you get paying clients.

If you cannot afford training, you can dedicate time to YouTube videos.

- *Analytic reports*: Another task is tracking and giving analytic reports to your clients. But first, what is an analytic report?

An analytic report is the number of metrics to be provided by you to show the performance (growth or maybe decline) of a client's social media account or page within a given time (monthly, for example).

There are usually four things to look out for:

Reach: This is the total number of accounts and pages that viewed your post. There is a difference between impression and reach. While I have just told you what Reach means, an impression means the total number of views on a particular post. You probably haven't seen the difference yet. Let me buttress it, one person can view a post twice or more. Impression count views (including the number of times one person viewed) while reach simply totals the number of people that viewed.

Interaction or Engagement: this is the number of people that engaged or interacted with a post or content by way of liking (or any other form of reaction), dropping a comment or even replying to comments, sharing the post, or saving it to watch later.

Page Likes or Follower Growth: This is how the growth of a page is measured and oftentimes, this is one of the key takeaway clients are interested in. Here, what is taken into account is how many page visits were recorded and how many people liked or followed the page. Note that page visit is not the same as page liking or following.

As a report, you need to have key performance indicators (KPIs) included for your clients. KPI is the factor that accounted for the results in your report. This could be a case of a Pandemic, November Black Friday sales, Political trends, December holidays, etc. All these may affect the performance of contents within given periods.

3. Social Media Marketer

This is the business part of social media management. This is about taking up jobs from individuals, small businesses, or corporate organizations that essentially target sales conversion. Here, marketers are required to make great offers that attract buyers and of course, they are expected to know how to use various marketing tools like ads, gathering customer avatars, competitive analysis, etc.

In essence, social media marketing is about creating offers on products or services and events that will drive in sales or signups.

This is because the main task of the social media manager is conversion. Knowledge of how to write sales copy and the skill of creating great sales offers is a great advantage.

Most social media marketers are Ads gurus. What that means is you cannot afford to not know how to run ads because you will need the skill to set up ads, get influencers' mentions if need be, and do promos, contests and giveaways.

Now, if you are still with me, you will understand why I had to show you the different variations in social media management. This is because, even though these three variations are separate, oftentimes, one person is hired for these 3 roles.

Would you blame clients? Most of them are unaware of which and what between the variations I showed you. I'm telling you about it so you can define your system and design your clientele packages accordingly before you onboard a client.

Getting Started

We have established that there is a space for you. Reiteratively, this space is created for you as a result of the inability of busy individuals and corporations to keep up with the demand for an active online presence. By this, it means they cannot keep up with the need to create and post content on their social media pages and handles and also to manage the engagements. If at all they do, there would be another difficulty that stems from their inability to be consistent.

Let me also state that most of these corporate organizations or personal brands will usually require graphical content to, apart from maintaining an active online presence, advertise and consolidate their brands. Oftentimes, they want content that market their unique value proposition or product differentiation.

The truth remains that these people or corporations not only know that they need an active online presence, but they also have a concise idea about the kind of content they need to achieve their social media objectives. Relax, I will teach you something about social media objectives later.

Does the question remain who would do all these for these individuals and corporate organizations?

You.

Now that you know the problem you have to help solve it. How best can you serve the solution? Don't start fidgeting yet. I am not about to ask you as many questions as I did in the other chapter.

Get Started

One thing you probably have wondered about is how to create content. I mean, you are wondering what to create content with. Most clients make available the information or resource material you would need for creating content on their social media pages or handles. If they won't, it will be an extra job for you.

Assuming you are not giving the information you will need, how do you go about this? Stick with me, I will show you.

Everything revolves around the need of individuals or corporate organizations. Clients' needs differ. Depending on the NEED of a client, you'd understand what exact service they need. I will talk about this in the next chapter.

One problem prevalent among many young social media managers is that they accept just any gig from clients without really assessing the need of the clients.

Let me give you a simple example:

Client A is a pastor who wants content created from the messages he preaches every Sunday (and scriptures) to inspire his followers about faith. Even though he leads a corporate organization, the church, he is an individual client. You must deal with him understanding whose need you are serving, the pastor or the church.

At the most basic level, you should know that the pastor's social media need differs from his church's social media need. Your job role should either be to serve the pastor's social media feed or the church's, not both unless you are assigned to undertake both job roles.

Client B is an HR company that tells you their core value proposition and leaves you to do complete handling of their social media page and make it active and engaging. This client's needs differ significantly.

Without any doubt, the need for Client B is more tasking. However, your job role will be to manage a corporate social media page.

You Don't Need Money to Start

I have said all these to help you understand, in the simplest way, that social media management is something anyone can do.

If you are reading this book and you are looking at the possibility of starting your social media

24

business, what you should begin to concern yourself with is how much time you have to spend online managing individuals' and corporate organizations' pages.

I won't lie to you. Your time is the primary capital you need to start this business, no doubt, but the truth is if you have knowledge or experience of how social media works, how the algorithm works, and how social media marketing and advertising work, it will be your greatest advantage.

Do you now see why I took out time, in the previous chapter, to teach you about analytics? To succeed in this business, you need to be a perpetual learner. You need to be updated about the latest policies and changes on various social media platforms to know what it affects. You would always need to be abreast with this information so that you can interpret its effects on your clients' businesses.

Sometimes, what you think is suitable for a page may not be proper for the client. This explains why you must learn and keep learning. You need to learn how content should be planned and how content strategy is developed.

Let me digress a bit. I will be back to continue on this.

You Need A Great Portfolio

One thing I strongly recommend you do is to take a certification course. Just before you start wondering why you would buy a book and the author is recommending that you should buy a course, wait and listen! When you finish reading this book, you won't get any certificates to show for it.

With a course, you get to be certified. You need to have a strong portfolio to attract the kind of clients that will pay the kind of money you dream of.

Talking about a great portfolio, can you get a website? It doesn't have to be a huge investment. Can you do a one-page website that welcomes your visitors and tell them what you do? Yes? Of course, it is possible. Somewhere on the page (I will suggest at the bottom), place a tab that links to an external payment gateway. Listen, all I am saying is that you need to look at it. Have an excellent portfolio.

26

There is Always This Constant

Just like any other business, financial capital may be available but that would not guarantee the success of the business. Knowledge will be required, too.

Wait a minute. In case you have not noticed, I am back from my digression.

There are many social media management agencies. You can do an internship with them. You don't have to ever meet with the CEOs or report in any office because it is always a remote job. The reason? You need to get knowledge. The internship will provide you with a *doing knowledge*. Yes, beyond social media management business in the pages of a book and video course, you will get acquainted with social media management business in practice.

As you are learning, you can create dummy accounts you can use to experiment with some things you are learning. In the last chapter of this book, you will be learning how the growth of social media pages is scaled, for now, use your dummy account to try out everything you would learn as an intern.

Listen to me. If you can draw your right ear to listen to me, I will love it. Do not assume you know this thing because you read a book and you took a course. The social media management business thrives on referrals. Don't disappoint your clients with the assumption you carry that you know how you can help them achieve their objectives.

Let me repeat it. Use dummy accounts, first. I will tell you why in the next chapter.

Do you now see that knowledge is always a constant?

Algorithm

Let me say this: this chapter is an addendum to the entire book. What you will find in this chapter is useful only to the degree that you see its usefulness in your journey as a social media manager.

Aside from High School, you're probably part of the people who would just hear about the algorithm for the first time in this book. I mentioned algorithm once in this book and that was in the section where I said *You Don't Need Money to Start* in **Chapter Three**. There, I said if you have a foreknowledge of what an algorithm is and how it works, you have an advantage.

What if you don't know what it is?

What if you don't know how it works?

Well, I thought I should give you a sneak peek.

The first thing you must bear in mind is that everything (or at least almost everything) I would share with you about the algorithm is subject to change. By this, I mean that you don't have to pick everything I would share hook, line, and sinker.

Why?

Because the algorithm is constantly changing.

Have you ever wondered why Meta has an office or at least what their staff does? They are constantly uncovering ways to ensure that every user is within check. Invariably, it means they are always working to make improvements.

The algorithm is what determines what is relevant and what is not.

The algorithm is what defines a user's interest, behaviour, and other attributes on a platform.

There are many things to be learned about algorithm but the first thing you need to know is that all social media platforms use algorithm. For this chapter, I will focus on Facebook though I may make mention of other platforms as the need arises.

Getting Started with Facebook

Have you observed that creating (registering) a new Facebook account is very simple? Yes, in just simple steps, you have your account created in seconds.

It's the same with most platforms. You create an account with ease but once the account is created, you won't be let to rest. You're reminded that your account setup is incomplete.

In some cases, you're denied access to a certain feature because your account setup is incomplete. Well, that's the algorithm trying to ensure that "you're paying for using their platform for free." Did this statement confuse you?

Don't be confused.

Facebook is not free. Yes, you heard that right. You're paying with your data. I don't mean your internet connection, I mean your information.

One thing most people don't do is that they don't

read the privacy policy of any platform or website before agreeing to and using it. Well, that's what you pay. They use your information.

This explains why they would constantly remind you to supply them with that information.

Why do you need to supply a platform your date of birth or your location?

Wait, Mark Z is not visiting you in your home. He's not about to call you to wish you a happy birthday. So, why does Mark's Facebook require you to give them this information?

They need it to make the money you're not paying them. Relax, they don't sell your information (at least, every privacy policy tells you so). They use it.

These are just a few basic records that the algorithm keeps about you. But the algorithm is so powerful. It knows what time of day you spend most online. It knows your favourite spots (pages you view most for example). It observes how you chat and it knows whether you pay more attention to either men or women. The algorithm knows lots of stuff.

So, whether you supply the information they need

from you after you signed up or not, they will still get other crucial information. I'm sorry I have to break this news but the truth is there is nothing you can do to stop the algorithm except if you never signed up on their platform in the first place. Remember, that's how you pay them for using their platform. Nothing is free after all.

Let me tell you something about numbers before we continue.

Numbers

Why does Facebook allow its users to have only 5,000 friends?

Simple.

5,000 is only good enough for fun and mutual social experience between friends who are connected irrespective of time and distance. But for business, 5,000 is such a poor number for marketing campaigns.

This is the difference between a Facebook account and a Facebook page. On a Facebook account, you're allowed to have a maximum of 5,000 friends while an unlimited number of followers are allowed on a Facebook page.

The interesting thing here is that Facebook uses its algorithm to ensure that when a post is made by an account, the post is shown to more than 10% of the account's total friends. For example, you have 4,120 friends. When you make a post, Facebook ensures that the post is distributed to the news feeds of at least 10% (412) of your friends. Though, not all of them will eventually see the post probably because they refreshed their news feeds before scrolling to your post.

When you make a post on your Facebook page, it is different altogether. A tiny minute of followers sees the post.

Ads

In chapter three, I equally mentioned that knowing about ads is an advantage. Interestingly, the reason why platforms collect and store information of and about their users is for ad purposes.

Ad means advertisement or advertising.

This is because the information Facebook collects will ensure accurate (not 100%) targeting. If

Facebook has your date of birth, it will send adverts that are targeted t people of your age bracket. Aside from the information they collect, they also use other information they have gathered from observing your interests and behaviour on their platform.

Just in case you're still wondering, how do you think Facebook penalizes people for violating certain standards?

Algorithm.

Let me show you how.

Words

At this point, I believe you know by now that the algorithm is high-level programming. Yeah, it is.

The algorithm takes note of certain words.

Remember, Facebook accounts are programmed in such a way that they support user experiences to become characterized by enjoyable social activities and fun experiences. Hence, it does not support marketing. Do you recall that I said a post made on a Facebook account is featured in about 10% of news feeds? I'm sure you do.

Now, you need to know that it is not just any post.

If the post is geared toward marketing, the algorithm frowns at it. By frowning, I mean it treats the post like it would a post on a page. A small number of friends (just like followers on a page) see the post in their news feed.

How does the algorithm know these posts?

The word used within the post.

Pay. Buy. Click. Link. Comment. Follow. These words and many more are frowned upon because they know you're looking for cheap traffic.

At the beginning of this chapter, I said the algorithm generally determines the post that is perceived to be relevant. Engagements (likes, comments, and shares) are some of the things the algorithm observes. Usually, the more engagements, the more the initial percentage allocated to a post is increased. In essence, the more people engage a post, the more that post is further featured in other news feeds.

There are other words that would flag your post too. By flag, I mean it sends a signal or an alarm on your post seeking that it should be reviewed immediately.

This is why a post can be live for up to five minutes before it is taken down by Facebook. It means something within the post flagged the post.

Vulgar Words

Sometimes the use of words like fight, sex, fuck off, what the fuck? and others that flag a post.

Interestingly, it is not limited to text only. Audio and video too.

How about copyright?

Assuming, you're using content that is not yours, especially a song, include the song title and or artist. If you don't know the song title and artist, simply acknowledge that you don't have a right to the song.

The algorithm is not always nice.

You probably have noticed that it no longer supports some third-party URLs especially shortened links especially bit.ly.

How to Beat Algorithm

A chapter is comprehensively dedicated to social media managers on beating the algorithm in such a way that it helps their work.

What I will share here is just a tip. Moreover, what works today may not work tomorrow because, as I have already said, the algorithm is constantly changing.

Already, I have told you about copyright.

Other ways would be how to use words.

If you needed to write *click*, you can write *cli.ck* instead.

This applies to other words too.

Fuck can be *Fvck* or *F**k*.

If you can avoid using these words completely, please do.

However, there's a way to solve some of these.

Instead of saying, "Kindly comment on my post," you can say "I will love to hear your view." That way, you have avoided using comment and post.

38

Instead of saying "Tell me what you think in the comment section," simply say "Does this makes sense to you?" or "Did you learn anything from this?"

I hope this chapter has given you an idea of how the algorithm works on social media. I will show you something different about influencing algorithms, follow me closely.

Learning On
The Job

This book is a store of knowledge and it is a guide in your hand. Beyond having capital (time) and the fundamental knowledge to get started, you will need some guidance.

Let's make some guides for you to work with it.

1. Identify your Nichè

How do you know your target clients? How do you know the client's target audience? It all starts with identifying a nichè that resonates with you. Your nichè should be narrowed to agree with your entire social media management business objective.

It is frustrating to jump into what you do not define and do not know so well. The keyword is your INTEREST.

If you like something, it is easier to create engaging posts on topics relating to it. It is difficult doing something that you do not have any emotional connection with. Sooner or later, it will become frustrating. The effect will be seen in your productivity level.

You must identify something you're passionate about and define your nichè around that thing. If it's an HR company's social media you want to manage, you need to have, at least, a little liking for anything HR and corporate organizations and interest in career success.

If you're the kind of person who detests corporate jobs and careers, it may be uneasy for you to create great contents that will suit corporate organizational needs.

This is because part of your job description will require you to read up or make research about HR and corporate organizational structures and more.

Note that I did not say it is impossible to manage pages of clients whose organizational objective you unlike or detest, I am saying it is uneasy. Because it is uneasy, it may affect your productivity level in execution.

If it's a church's page or a pastor's social media page/account, you must be a Christian, at least. That way, you can handle the task and deliver it appropriately.

If it's a food processing industry and food happens not to be something you are interested in, you must know about diet and nutrition and this can only come from a place of research.

Even if you don't know much about it, you need to have room within you to be willing to know. Find a way to subject your body to be willing to make research. This one is going to be something you would do all the time, whether it is your nichè or not, the difference is that research outside your nichè is going to be more tasking than the one in your nichè.

When you clearly define your interest and identify

43

your nichè, it makes it easy to know your target clients. There is no harm in turning down job offers. You must not work with every client.

Working for a client whose needs do not contravene with your beliefs and interest makes it easy for you to run a profitable social media management business.

2. Create your Online Business Page

It starts with creating a Facebook Page and an Instagram Business Account. Truth is, most clients won't hire you until they request to see proof of competence – your business account. Do you now see why I asked you to create dummy accounts? Your page has to look it. Your page needs to have a voice to tell prospective clients that you are able.

What is my bias for mentioning Facebook and Instagram? Nothing. There is no bias. However, they often would top the list of most job offers you would get.

So, when clients request to see your business account, what they want to see is not just your ownership of a business account. Actually, by

44

seeing your business account, they can see how many pages you are managing at the moment.

Does that mean you would only have your dummy pages to show?

Don't you think some clients want to see a page they can verify?

Truth is, nobody wants to be a sacrificial lamb. I mean, nobody wants to be used as an experiment. It's like a fresh graduate seeking a job, the most challenging problem he faces is employers are asking for "job experience," – jobs in companies or organizations they can verify.

It's the same thing...

Clients want to see your "job experience" by asking to see your business account.

Not to worry, I will show you how to close the gap and deal with this job experience challenge in this book.

Once I show you how to sort this challenge, the next thing you would need is a referral. That could be a challenge too but I will show you how to move to pass it.

3. Find your Test Clients

You probably noted that I said most prospective clients will request to see proof of previous jobs before they engage you, right? Allow me to let you in on how to close the gap.

It is important to note that it is a display of wisdom to start your social media management business with test clients.

Who are test clients?

Your test clients could be your pastors, mentors, friends, family, leaders, etc. You can offer to manage their social media pages (or handles) since they're people whom you have some kind of relationship with and you perceive that they are busy people.

Whatever the case, you need these test clients for two reasons:

i. Grow your competence

ii. Have proof of competence

Test clients don't mean free clients in the actual sense but if you are having difficulty getting those that wish to pay a little fee, I will advise that you should still go ahead and do it for free for a short time.

However, set clear boundaries between you and your test clients. Let them know why you're doing it for such A LITTLE FEE OR FREE and why you're doing it for such A SHORT TIME. That is because when the big and very engaging clients come knocking, you may have to shove aside their jobs under the carpet unless they are willing to either increase the fee or start paying a fee.

While you're doing it, get all analytic reports that show progress. Ensure you always note the most engaging posts. Find the reasons for the engagements. The reasons could be because the post was funny, informative, or motivational.

If it is a free client, you can use the report you're getting on his or her page to bid for a "small fee." Well, bidding for this fee is not compulsory, you have to use your discretion.

More importantly, the report is important for you at that period because it is going to be the

47

achievement you will add to your job experience when new clients request to see your account for proof.

4. Create Your Package

It is one thing to define a client's need by clearly defining the job role or roles (engager, manager or marketer, or both), it is another thing to ascertain how many contents per week or day in a month, and the fee (charge)? Yes, you need to have all these sorted.

For example, 5 contents in a week. Approximately 20 contents for ₦25,000 (monthly).

But again, what is the nature of the content?

If you receive ₦25,000 (monthly), it means you are paid about ₦1,200 per content. Therefore, you should note that you are creating your packages based on the nature of the content you are required to create.

Graphic illustrations and videos take a long time and creativity. They require definite skills.

I am saying all these so you will understand your

package will determine whether you are adequately paid or underpaid.

Competence grows. As you grow, you can turn your business into an agency and create packages that, rather than charge on monthly basis, charge per content.

5. Create Your System

Creating a system is not necessarily meant for starters. This is because a system is useful mainly for those who are already managers of social media pages and are looking for means to scale their social media management business into an agency.

A system is required to define how you reach agreements with clients before you onboard them.

With a system, you can create questionnaires for your clients. Questionnaires are like structures that help you serve your clients with custom-made service needs which meet their social media page needs.

You also need systems that help you define the kind of questions you should ask your client or the files (data) to request from them for content creation.

This applies to big clients like companies or businesses. That is how you know your client's target audience or market.

One of the most important things you must request from your clients so that you can serve them better is that they state what their social media objectives are. That way, you will be able to measure milestones and note landmarks in your business.

You will also need a system that helps you know the tools you will need to create a content calendar such that you never have to run dry of ideas for content creation.

Social media management tools like CoSchedule, Hootsuite, Later, and Tailwind can help you facilitate your job and standardize your social media management business but they are not free.

However, I stated those tools so you would know that you would need once you start getting paying clients. In the mean time, there are tools like Buffer whose free plan is great especially when you are starting out with test clients.

At the time of writing this book, Buffer allows three platforms (to host two channels each) for free. for example, LinkedIn is a platform. On one platform, you can have two channels (LinkedIn Page and Linkedin account).

Since Buffer free plan is limited, you can use Business Suite to complement Buffer. Its free.

You can install 'Business Suite' from Playstore on your phone and use it to manage Facebook and Instagram. it works for Facebook and Instagram only because it owned by Meta. It is a great tool because it can host as many Facebook and Instagram pages as possible.

Chapter 6

Landing Yourself
A Job

Apart from test clients whose social media pages or handles are an experiment, you need to land yourself a paying gig – a job from a paying client. You need to begin by having a simple practice. Let your followers on social media know what you do. How do I mean? Brand yourself.

You need to be seen making content and posting on your media accounts and pages talking about your clients and the result they are getting than you do about yourself or your personal life. Oh hold on, I am not against you making content and posting about your personal life, it should be less than you do about your clients.

Nobody emerges from the blues and gets people to invest their trust in him in a flash. Brand awareness is about building trust. Let me say it again, show up daily and say something about what you do, how it is benefitting your clients, and how you are equally ready to help them with their social media management needs.

Remember, if you don't have a paying client yet, you have a test client. A client is still a client, paying or testing.

Make a Research

On various social media pages, use the search tab to make searches. What are you searching for? Organizations and individual brands.

You have to define a niche or an interest, it is your premium guide to the keywords you would use.

Let us assume you are interested in animal production and agriculture. Weird, right? The weirdest the example, the better your understanding.

Go to Facebook and tap on the search tab. Type in words like:

Animal production

Animal production technology

Animal health and production

Animal Science

Farms and consults

Agro and consults

Etc.

The list is endless.

Search for each keyword in the 'Pages' category. From the pages' names you find, ensure you copy the name titles and do a further search on each of them. Check them out on Google. Yes, check them out on Linkedin, Twitter, Instagram, etc.

What would you be looking out for?

Are they consistent in making and posting content on their pages?

Just find a pitfall.

Once you do, send a DM or an email. You can send a DM from social media, you can send an email through their website (this is why I said you should check them out on Google to find their website).

In your message, tell them what you can help them do base on the pitfall you found, let them know how you have helped other brands (only you know they were test pages) with similar problems and the result (be specific) they got.

Do this for as many pages as you can.

Stay Glued to Pages

On Instagram, search and follow:

@tribecalledena

@theefficientbusinessteam

@socialmediaguru_ng

Facebook too

@Digital Marketing Institute

@Social Media Examiner

@RJ Media Consults

These selected social media handles are social media

managers. Stay glued to them, some of them share about social media jobs.

You can follow Jobberman on all social media platforms as they share job openings.

You might just be lucky.

Connect

You have to learn to connect with other social media managers. Besides being an intern for some social media management agencies, you can also create a connection to the end that jobs can be given to you.

How do I mean?

Let us assume you did an internship at Ezra Media Agency last year. Now you are independent. If you were good with roles assigned to you while you were an intern and you maintained a great working relationship with them.

Don't you think when they have a client they cannot onboard because their hands are full, they would want to recommend someone?

That person should be you. Do what it takes to be

that person that gets recommended.

Secondly, because you don't have the experience they have in the business, what happens when you land yourself in trouble with a client? This is why you must connect with existing agencies.

Chapter 7

Scale Your Own Business

If you're reading this chapter, count yourself lucky and I will tell you why.

Only the revised version of this book has this chapter added to it. I call it an updated version not because I changed anything that is already in the book but because this particular chapter is an addendum. After you're done reading, you may want to call it a sequel. The difference between an addendum and a sequel is something I don't know. Anyone that fits, use it.

Let's assume you now have a business, a social media management business, how do you get the business to fly fast? Note: this chapter is not for the amateur. Hitherto, this book is written for those who want to start, and that's for an amateur.

You have to be ready for business; I mean you have to be ready and prepared to build a thriving social media management business, to get the most of this chapter. That's something way above amateurs.

This chapter is so important. From the previous chapters, I have already shown you how you can start the business and create your own system, right?

You can start by doing it free. I remember mentioning this. But more than this, I also remember mentioning that some prospective clients will ask to see some results before they give a deal to you. By result, it is not about the number of social media pages you're managing only, but how much you have been able to grow these pages. Your inability to present proof of results will impede every system you create from working.

Apart from everything you already know about page growth, let me be a bit realistic with you.

60

Assuming I have a page and you decide to help me manage the page for free. You can almost be sure that you won't be able to tell me to give you money to pay for ads so that the page can grow.

So, what would you do? This is what this chapter is about.

I will share two things:

Recruit Commenters

As it is right now, we have a lot of "jobless people" on social media who would do anything for money. Anything that promises a dividend on money they spend to buy data to be on social media and the time they also spend chatting and doing all sorts of stuff on social media is something people will rush at.

Let me show you some examples.

Opera News does something similar. They get people to write and post news articles. All they are required to do is to sign up and creat their news hub account, they create content (news articles) and post them, manage their stats based on the performance of every news article they post. They are then paid based on the performance of every news article they post.

How about the Hawkit app? A lot of people are joining it because it pays them for doing one thing or the other. For example, people on Hawkit are paid for performing various tasks on social media including likes and comments, shares and referrals. Referrals on adverts or posts of people's products are also remunerated based on products purchases through people's referral links.

I hope these examples I have given you are already forming into some ideas already?

Either way, there are two lessons to be learned here.

1. People are onboarded into a system to perform certain tasks.

2. The people get rewarded, not for performing the said task, but based on the performance of the task they perform. This means that a person may perform a task but the task may in turn not perform well. Hence, he is paid based on how the task turned out not because he did his part by

performing the task.

But then, how does this connect to social media management?

Follow me closely.

Imagine you design a simple system that on-boards interested people as commenters. For every post you make on different social media pages or accounts, they go there and make comments. Remember, commenters will not be paid because they simply made comments under a post but rather, they will get paid based on the performance of the comments they make.

Why? You may ask.

If any comment is the thing, a commenter will just drop any comment and expect to be paid. This means the comment may be so irrelevant and not constructive and yet expects to be paid. Hence, there has to be a system that measures the relevance of every comment.

Note that what suggests the relevance of a post in the context of growing a social media page is not just about how critical of the content a commenter is or the intellectual disposition of the commenter. On social media, the perception that a content is performing well is gauged on the metrics of engagement it generates.

Therefore, every commenter must be told or taught to craft comments that are strong enough to generate reactions (replies).

What is the advantage of using commenters?

Yes, why do you need commenters? To influence social media algorithm. In simple terms, it means that the more people comment on a post, the more the system that controls the social media platform you are using ensures that the post is further shown to more people. If the initial number of people the post is shown to when it was posted was 20, by the time 5 people make comments on the post, the social media algorithm will ASSUME that the content of that post is relevant and so it will deem fit to be further shown to more people.

Let me reiterate, if you have 20 people whom you recruit as commenters and let them know that they are not just paid for making meaningful comments on a post, that won't be a bad idea though, but that they would be paid for the replies their comment generates. By implication, they are paid for the PERFORMANCE of their comments.

The implication is that every commenter will be intentional about their comments and also ensure that they do their best to make sure their comments on your post generate replies because that is how they get paid.

Well, some of these commenters are smart. They too will onboard their family and friends to reply to their comments on your post so that they get to be paid by you. In the long run, it is a win-win situation if you look at it critically.

What you want is engagements (likes, and comments and comment replies). Either way, you have gotten what you want. What a commenter wants is to be paid, if getting people to do his bid so he can get paid is in line with achieving the overarching objective, let him be paid. It is a win-win.

Someone may probably say this is going to be more effective than using social media ads. I don't think so. I will tell you why.

The power of social media ads is the ability it has to target specific audience with a sharp precision. Using commenters does not have the ability to target specific audience.

Are you beginning to think that this is too serious for you? You make me laugh.

A business is a serious business. Yes... If you call it social media management business, then it is a serious business. You have to get serious too.

Wait... How did you think some people were able to make a fortune out of this? It's not luck. It is by meeting up with the seriousness required.

So, how do you onboard commenters?

Make a simple post on your WhatsApp status or Facebook page or any social media platform you are on. For example: "What do you think about making some cool cash by just making comments on social media? If you're interested, click this link to register for free."

Before you start wondering who's going to pay the commenters, let me tell you now. It's you. Yes, you. Do not onboard more recruiters than you can pay from your pocket. But you have to pay.

How do they register?

Create a form online. You can use a simple Google form forms.google.com or Cognito form www.cognitoforms.com

The bottom line is that it gives you access to their emails. You can always send them emails containing the links to posts you make on any page so they can go straight to the post and make their comments.

On the form, ensure you explain to them what they are about to sign up for. Secondly, ensure they receive a confirmation message from you which also breaks down every detail. The details of when they get to receive their payment (how long it needs to accrue), could be weekly or bi-weekly; it could be a benchmark like their funds must reach a certain threshold before they can request for withdrawal (which means the money to be sent to them).

Lastly, you need to create a system that helps you

update them. For example, on weekly basis, they get to receive a different email that tells them how many replies their comments (specific comments) on different generated. This is why you must learn to use social media insight very well.

Let me be honest with you. Social media management business is something you can do from the comfort of your home, they say, but you cannot be comfortable at this level of the business. There is usually so much work to be done here.

Whether at home or not, you have to bring yourself to work and be guided by office hours. When I said office hours, I don't mean a physical office environment, you have to work with the consciousness of being a business person who resumes work daily at a particular time of the day and closes at another hour of the day.

Make Group Posts on Facebook

Not many people know that a Facebook business page can join a group or groups on Facebook.

When you're opening a new page, you're being greeted with some group suggestions. In other words, Facebook makes suggestions for you to join some pages.

Aside from this, you can also join different groups with the different pages you are managing. Just ensure that the different groups you're joining are relevant in some ways to the individual pages you are managing. That way, you can also share the post you create in these groups.

You may not need your commenters to go into these groups to make comments but if you're like me who's not calm and patient when I'm pursuing results, you can involve them to make comments in posts you make in groups too.

Let me say this again. I don't sweet-talk and cajole. I just tell you what I think is best or what I think can work. If you're ready to scale this business, be ready to put in the work. You're lucky you have the content of this book to guide you.

Not many of us had access to a good resource like this book to guide us even when we are willing to pay. Yes, we didn't find good resources to buy. It is what we have tried and learned in the process you are reading from with ease.

But why do I always digress? No more digression. I will just stop here.

Chapter
8

Just One Advice
For You

It's an advice. You should see it as one.

Learn to be current and updated. Almost every information shared in this book is transient.

While the Social Media Management business is something that has come to stay, and yes it has come to stay, the practices wouldn't remain the same.

The common frequent changes stem from policy changes. Let me be honest with you, anything can change. In fact, everything will change in the course of time.

Ads policies, for example, are constantly being

improved. Some changes that come with these improvements will require you to make certain adjustments

Let me give you an example. I was already done with writing this book when I discovered the update on Facebook that users flip their account and their page. That is, access to pages requires a flip from an account (which temporarily logs out the account) to allow the page function like an account. Before this time, I had stated in the book that it is impossible to search and join groups on a page while using a smart phone. On this discovery, I had to update the book.

You might be wondering what is special in this last chapter and in the advice I have stated. The only special message here is that in whatever you do, ensure you don't lag behind until you're lagged out of the business. You sharpen your edge every time you don't miss out on changes made in any social media platform.

I'm done with the advice.

CONCLUSION

Like its name implies, it is media (channels) of socialization. This is why each social medium (like Facebook, Tiktok, etc.) has a reason for its establishment.

If social media was a location where anyone could go and receive money, everyone would be cashing out from it, but it is not so.

The book unveiled why an online business as this one - social media management can be conducted in real time by exploiting the advantage of the social media platform. It explains what social media management business is about, and guides its reader on the processes to set up a social media management business.

Everything this book has done is to simplify the socomplex social media management business into simple chewable tablets.

I am believing that you can now find the spot where you can start your social media business.

With everything you have read, if starting a social media management business still looks difficult in your sight, what you need to do is simple.

Just start.

Take the first step. Then the second step. And then the next... One step at a time. You would conquer it all.

MEET THE AUTHOR

Ezra Danjuma Akama is a transformational speaker, serial author, founder of Emerge 360° Africa, and the Principal Partner of Emergence Publishers.

He is the project coordinator of Rural Oral Health Campaign. A nonprofit program which promotes oral health among rural residents.

Ezra is a lifelong learner and an educator. Being a tech and soft skill enthusiast, he has educated young African Millennials in the last 4 years across different physical and virtual platforms. Ezra has trained over 10,000 young people in Nigeria, Cameroon, Ghana, The Gambia, South Africa, Sierra Leone, Liberia, Burundi and other African countries south of the Sahara.

He is presented with award of recognition from

Progressive Youth Organisation in Sierra Leone, Youths World Organisation in Cameroon among others. Ezra has also been featured on radio Mega FM (Warri, Nigeria).

Ezra has key interest in digital skills, business development, education and writing.

Ezra is a published author of both print and eBooks. Ezra is also a book project consultant.

Currently, Ezra is undergoing mentorship with Elisha Mamman International and Club10 Network. Ezra is also a member of the Fela Durotoye Leadership Network.

Ezra is a certified Public Speaker. He has also earned himself many other certificates from other endeavours too many mention.

Connect with Ezra

+234 (0)806 642 9711

ezradanjuma@gmail.com

Ezra Danjuma Akama

facebook.com/theezradanjuma

instagram.com/theezradanjuma

@theezradanjuma

Ezra Danjuma Akama

Who says you have to be a writer to have a book? While writing is the mountain standing between some people and authoring a book, the hindrance for others is the imagination that publishing is a difficult technical process.

This book – Self Publishing, from its title, should allay your fears. You can start your journey to becoming an author without ever needing a traditional publisher.

In this book, everything you need – how to generate profitable book ideas, tips on idea documentation (even without having to actually write), publishing tools, and marketing, is fully explained.

To get this book, go to https://selar.co/qe9m

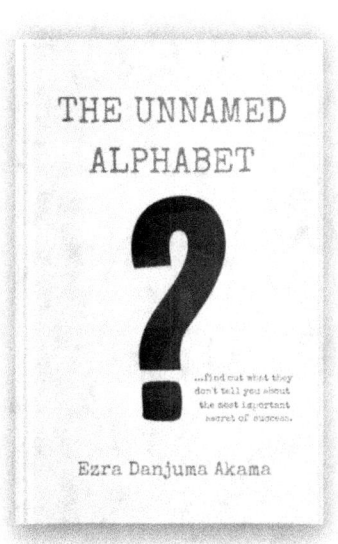

**THE UNNAMED
ALPHABET**

...find out what they
don't tell you about
the most important
secret of success.

Ezra Danjuma Akama

It is true that every successful person developed defiance to fear, especially the type that stops people from taking risk but they were never always like that.

The one most important ability they all developed is have courage and stay confident. They couldn't have been consistent without having courage and being confident.

This is what this book is about. It teaches how to find your power of confidence, develop it and safeguard it. You need confidence in yourself, in your actions and in your beliefs to stay focused and get every desired result come to fruition.

To get this book, go to https://selar.co/v8wm

Every human is uniquely made by God to carry out a precise assignment or fulfil a definite purpose on the earth. You will not be able to carry out this assignment if you are not introduced to your unique abilities and gift.

In this book, you would find worksheet that will help you to unmask and find the gift(s) you are equipped with by God and discover the assignment God wants you carry out using the gift as the tools you need.

You have a place in the creation and you have a task to play to reclaim dominion and enforce the purposes of God on the earth.

To order, https://selar.co/jkgv or +234 (0) 806 642 9711